Everett Railroad:
History Through the Miles

Barton Jennings

Everett Railroad: History Through the Miles
Copyright © 2018 by Barton Jennings

All rights reserved. This book may not be duplicated or transmitted in any way, or stored in an information retrieval system, without the express written consent of the publisher, except in the form of brief excerpts or quotations for the purpose of review. Making copies of this book, or any portion, for any purpose other than your own, is a violation of United States copyright laws.

Publisher's Cataloging-in-Publication Data
Jennings, Barton

Everett Railroad: History Through the Miles
58p.; 21cm.
ISBN: 978-0-9849866-9-9

Library of Congress Control Number: 2018943438

First Edition

Front cover photo by Barton Jennings
Back cover image courtesy of the Everett Railroad

Please send comments or corrections to sarah@techscribes.com

TechScribes, Inc.
PO Box 620
Avon, IL 61415
www.techscribes.com

Printed in the United States of America

*for the friends who have ridden
my excursion trips over the years*

Other books by this author:

Arkansas & Missouri Railroad: History Through the Miles
Alaska Railroad: History Through the Miles
Iowa Interstate Railroad: History Through the Miles
Tennessee Central Railway: History Through the Miles

Contents

Preface 6

Everett Railroad – Current Operations 7

Everett Railroad History 15

Morrison's Cove Branch 17

    Duncansville Wye to Brookes Mills................................21

    Brookes Mills to Henrietta...31

Martinsburg Branch 45

Bedford Secondary...49

About the Author...57

Preface

This guide is not designed to be a complete history of the Everett Railroad, but instead it provides a great deal of information for those who like to ask, "Where are we and what once happened here?" Because of this, the guide includes information about current as well as former station locations, historic towns, and major stream crossings along the line.

This route description was first written about 2010 for several visits to the Everett Railroad. It was rewritten several years later for a special charter train operated as a retirement party for a good friend. Requests for copies of the guide resulted in this book.

Much of the information comes from internal railroad records, government and public records, railroad workers, and conversations with old and new friends. It is hoped that you enjoy your adventure with the Everett Railroad and that this book will be of assistance in some ways – *Everett Railroad: History Through the Miles*.

Everett Railroad – Current Operations

The Everett Railroad Company (EV) is a Class III short line operating from a connection with Norfolk Southern at Hollidaysburg, south through Blair County in the Allegheny Mountains region of Pennsylvania. The railroad operates 23 route miles of track and serves industries such as feed mills, a paper mill, lumber, and several transload facilities. The railroad handles freight cars weighing as much as 263,000 pounds, more than three times the weight of a large semi-truck, removing thousands of trucks off of local roads each year. The Everett Railroad is a member of the American Short Line and Regional Railroad Association (ASLRRA) and is a repeat winner of the ASLRRA's Jake Award for safety.

The Everett Railroad was until recently technically three different operations. The first was the Everett Railroad, which operated Brookes Mills to Sproul. The second operation was the Morrison's Cove Railroad from Roaring Spring to Martinsburg. At first, the Everett Railroad leased the Morrison's Cove Railroad. It was purchased by and merged into the Everett Railroad in 2013. The third operation was the Hollidaysburg & Roaring Spring Railroad (H&RS). The H&RS was a combination of leased track and trackage rights between Hollidaysburg and Roaring Spring. In January 2015, the H&RS was merged into the Everett Railroad. This brought all of the current 23 miles of Everett-operated trackage under one corporate name. All traffic from the lines is interchanged with Norfolk Southern at Hollidaysburg.

The modern Everett Railroad provides service to about a dozen customers on its line between Hollidaysburg and Brookes Mills, and then the two branches to Sproul and Martinsburg. Freight trains normally operate Monday, Wednesday and Friday, but they often run based upon the needs of the railroad's customers. Commodities handled include paper; wood pulp; lumber; feed ingredients; chemicals and slurries for papermaking; and bauxite ore. The Everett Railroad moves on average 2,000 railcars a year.

Over the past four years, Everett Railroad has reinvested close to $1 million in the railroad, all private funds. Improvements have included the purchase of a portion of the Hollidaysburg rail yard from Norfolk Southern; the construction of switches and yard tracks; the construction of an entrance road to the property; and the construction of a new maintenance shop and related track work at Duncansville.

PASSENGER TRAIN RIDES

The Everett Railroad operates a number of unique passenger train trips from its new Hollidaysburg station to multiple destinations and for multiple events. Passenger excursion service, often behind steam locomotive #11, operates many weekends during tourist season. Some of these trips include *Family Train Rides* to Brookes Mills, *Ice Cream Specials* to Roaring Spring, and *Steam Into Morrison's Cove* trips to Martinsburg. *Pumpkin Patch Specials* run to Kladder during the Halloween season, while *Santa's Express* trips head to Brookes Mills for Christmas, providing holiday entertainment. A number of other trains run for other special events, so check out the railroad's website for details.

Everett #11 (2-6-0) at Hollidaysburg station. Photo by Sarah Jennings.

Current Operations

PASSENGER CARS

Currently, the Everett Railroad uses five passenger cars on its excursion trains. Combine #23 was built in 1925 for the Bessemer & Lake Erie Railroad by the Pressed Steel Car Company of Pittsburgh, Pennsylvania. During the 1950s, the car became part of the business car train as diner A-200. It eventually was retired and donated to the Pennsylvania Trolley Museum in 1964 and acquired by the Everett Railroad in 2012.

Combine #23, former Bessemer & Lake Erie A-200, is shown in excursion service in 2016. Photo by Sarah Jennings.

Office car 912 was built in 1906 for the Baltimore & Ohio Railroad. The B&O sold it to a group of Titusville businessmen in 1960, and the car was used as a clubhouse, located next to the Pennsylvania Railroad's Buffalo – Pittsburgh main line. After the last owner died, the car was sold to the Pittsburgh & Shawmut Railroad. In 1995, the car was bought by Alan Maples and moved to the Everett Railroad.

Office car #912 is shown at Kladder in 2016. Photo by Sarah Jennings.

The railroad also currently uses three former Delaware, Lackawanna & Western (DL&W) cars that once operated as Multiple-Unit (MU) cars, providing commuter service out of Hoboken, New Jersey. The coaches were once self-powered, using electricity from overhead wires. These cars, #103, #104, and #105, are leased from the Horseshoe Curve Chapter of the National Railway Historical Society in Altoona. The cars, former Erie Lackawanna 3501 (DL&W 2501), 3537 (DL&W 2537), and 3533 (DL&W 2533) have had their traction motors and pantographs removed.

Car #103 is a typical commuter coach. Photo by Sarah Jennings.

In early 2018, a former Pittsburgh & Lake Erie (P&LE) coach was moved to the Everett Railroad from the Pittsburgh Station Square complex. This complex was the former P&LE passenger facility serving Pittsburgh. The car is a 70-foot coach built by the Pressed Steel Car Company.

Several other passenger cars are also on the property, owned by the railroad. These include two former Central Railroad of New Jersey (CNJ) commuter coaches (#1183 and #1198), both built by the Standard Steel Car Company.

LOCOMOTIVES

The Everett Railroad operates freight service with four diesel-electric locomotives. Passenger service is provided by both the diesels and steamer #11.

Current Operations

Diesel Locomotives

#561 is a General Electric B32-8. It was built in 1989 as Norfolk Southern #3561. It was renumbered #561 in 2015, retired in 2015, and sold to the Everett Railroad in 2017.

#707 is an Electro-Motive Diesel (EMD) GP9 built for the Illinois Central (IC). The IC rebuilt it into a GP10 at their Paducah Shops (KY) in the early 1970s. It operated for Illinois Central Gulf, Gulf & Mississippi, MidSouth Railroad, and Qwest Communications. It was originally built in 1956 and acquired by the Everett Railroad in 2004.

#1712 is an EMD GP7 built in 1950 as Clinchfield #911. It was rebuilt into a GP16 by the Seaboard Coast Line in 1981. It was later owned by CSX and RJ Corman before being bought by the Everett Railroad in 2002.

#1828 is a sister to #1712. It was also built as a GP7, this time as Seaboard Air Line #1978. It was also rebuilt into a GP16 (#4782) by the Seaboard Coast Line in 1981. It was later owned by CSX and RJ Corman before coming to the Everett Railroad in 2001.

Everett 1828 is parked near the shops at Duncansville. Photo by Barton Jennings.

The Everett Railroad also still owns General Electric 80-ton #4. This small locomotive was built in 1943 and was acquired in 1971. While it no longer is used for freight service, #4 is the oldest non-steam locomotive on the railroad and is the last piece of equipment on the current roster that dates back to the original Everett Railroad.

Steam Locomotives

Steam locomotive #11 was built in 1920 by the Cooke Works of the American Locomotive Company in Paterson, New Jersey. This ALCO 2-6-0 (Mogul) was originally intended to be exported to Cuba, but was sold to the Narragansett Pier Railroad in Peace Dale, Rhode Island, in 1923. It was resold in 1937 to the Bath & Hammondsport Railroad. #11 was retired in 1949, and eventually sold in 1955 to Dr. Stanley A. Groman and his *Rail City* museum in Sandy Pond, NY. After the museum's closure, #11 then went back to the Narragansett Pier Railroad about 1977, but was never restored or operated. It was again sold in 1981, going to the Middletown & New Jersey Railroad of Middletown, NY. #11 was stored and protected, again not operated, and went to James Wright, and then Alan Maples, president of the Everett Railroad, in 2006. #11 was rebuilt in the shops of the Western Maryland Scenic Railroad and then finished at the Everett Railroad's shop in Claysburg. The steamer returned to service during the fall of 2015 and regularly operates on the excursion train.

This photo clearly shows the 2-6-0 wheel arrangement of Everett #11. Photo by Barton Jennings.

Current Operations

Everett #11 pulls a passenger train through Hollidaysburg. Photo by Sarah Jennings.

Steam locomotive #38 dates back to the original Huntingdon & Broad Top Mountain Railroad & Coal Company. It was built in April 1927 by the Baldwin Locomotive Works. It is a 2-8-0, or Consolidation steamer. #38, and its identical sister #37, were the last new locomotives bought by the H&BTM. #38 was the last operable locomotive of the railroad and was used to scrap the railroad. #38 was originally considered for purchase by the Everett Railroad, but the company decided on a more modern diesel. When retired, #38 was acquired by Dr. Stanley Groman for his *Rail City* operation through Pittsburgh Rail and Machinery, along with a coach, RPO and a cabin car. Being too large for the excursion railroad, #38 was sold to the Livonia, Avon & Lakeville Railroad in 1968. It operated on excursions until 1976. It then went to the Gettysburg Railroad, owned by Sloan Cornell. It later went to the Knox & Kane Railroad. It was finally sold at auction to Alan Maples, president of the Everett Railroad. It is being rebuilt as time allows.

Everett Railroad: History Through the Miles

Everett #11 (2-6-0) under steam in Hollidaysburg. Photo by Sarah Jennings.

Everett Railroad History

The Everett Railroad's corporate history dates back to 1953, when the Huntingdon & Broad Top Mountain Railroad started their abandonment. A number of shippers and community leaders in the Everett area joined together to buy the southernmost four miles of the railroad, which connected to the Pennsylvania Railroad (PRR). The Everett Railroad began operations on April 1, 1954. The railroad's first locomotive was a Whitcomb 65-ton center cab internal combustion locomotive, acquired from the Conemaugh & Black Lick at Johnstown (PA), although steam was considered.

The 1950s were tough years for the railroad industry. The railroads' revenues were under attack by the construction of the Interstate Highway System, recessions in 1953 and 1958, and the start of the jet age. Railroads were saddled with obsolete work rules, massive passenger deficits, and restrictive regulation. Because of this, a number of railroads entered bankruptcy while others were totally abandoned. Although dieselization and other technology developments were signs of hope, the slide to the railroad crisis of the late 1960s and early 1970s had begun. Because of this, few railroads were started in the 1950s. Most lines that were started in that period, like the Everett, were efforts to save lines that were threatened with abandonment.

The first five years of the Everett were successful. Revenues grew from $70,000 in 1955 to $114,000 in 1960. The railroad was profitable and paid dividends. In 1961, things turned gloomy for the Everett Railroad as the company's largest customer, Tatesville Silica, closed. To try to save the railroad, steam-powered passenger excursion service began on Memorial Day in 1965, using former Morehead & North Fork 2-6-2 #11. The passenger business failed to restore profitability. In 1968, the Everett had about $36,000 in revenues; $25,000 from moving freight, and $11,000 from the 9,000 passengers that rode the excursion service. However, the railroad lost $8,000 that year. The railroad exited the excursion business in 1971 and sold the passenger equipment to the Williams Grove Park and Historical Society of Pennsylvania.

Everett Railroad: History Through the Miles

Hurricane Agnes destroyed the Pennsylvania Railroad track toward Cumberland in 1972, cutting off the Baltimore & Ohio as an option for the freight off of the Everett Railroad. This forced all traffic to go north through Hollidaysburg, not always the fastest or lowest cost route. In the late 1970s and early 1980s, Conrail began abandoning many lightly used branchlines, and the Bedford Secondary was no exception. In October 1982, Conrail abandoned the line and the Everett Railroad was cut off and abandoned.

In 1984, new owners, including Alan Maples, purchased the existing shares of the Everett, and bought the tracks between Brookes Mills and Sproul, setting up their new shops and headquarters in Claysburg. The initial customers were Champion Homes and General Refractories. The following year, the Everett Railroad leased the Morrison's Cove Railroad, which owned the southernmost six miles of the ex-Conrail Cove Branch, between Roaring Spring and Curryville. The final step in creating today's Everett Railroad was the purchase of the line between Hollidaysburg and Roaring Spring, done through the subsidiary Hollidaysburg & Roaring Spring Railroad. In 2013, the Morrison's Cove Railroad was acquired by the Everett Railroad, and the Hollidaysburg & Roaring Spring Railroad was absorbed in 2015, creating a unified Everett Railroad.

Morrison's Cove Branch

The Morrison's Cove Branch has had a number of names over the years. Among some of the most reported are the Hollidaysburg and Morrison's Cove branch, Morrison's Cove Railroad, and the Martinsburg Branch. No matter the name, the goal of the line was to serve the farm-based businesses in Morrison's Cove, as well as the iron mines and other industries along the route.

In 1933, Reverend C. W. Karns published the book *Historical Sketches of Morrisons Cove*. It starts off with the following statement.

> There is a legend that the "Cove", or "Covert", was used in early days as a hiding place for stolen horses by a man named Morris who was a notorious horse-thief in the eastern counties of Pennsylvania, and when pursued brought his stolen animals here for safe keeping.

However, the Reverend then stated that there was no real record of where the name came from. It was noted that the valley had a long history of rich farming and raising livestock. The supply of nearby timber in the mountains and plenty of water added the ability to build homes and mills to process the products from the farms.

Records over the years show a number of versions of the name, including Morrisons Cove, Morrison Cove or Morrison's Cove. Several sources conflict with the history of Reverend C. W. Karns and state that the "Great Cove" or "Big Cove" were names given to the area by the Indians, and that it was named "Morrisons Cove" for surveyor James Morrison in 1770.

The rail line into the Cove was built by the Pennsylvania Railroad (PRR) in 1871-72. Reports state that the line was built by the contractors Thomas and Collins, with Colonel John A. Lemon heading up the construction. All of these people were well known in the railroad construction business. James McCrea of Philadelphia was credited with the line's engineering. James McCrea was later president of the Pennsylvania Railroad (1907 to 1913). Newspapers of the time report that the line opened for traffic on May 6, 1872. The newspapers stated that the line tapped "a thickly settled manufacturing and agricultural country." Newspapers described the opening celebration and route, hosted by the railroad on a ten-car excursion train from Martinsburg to Altoona and back on that date. The excursion train departed Martinsburg at 8am and arrived at Hollidaysburg at 9am, and then after a celebration, arrived at Altoona at 11am. The train quickly turned, picked up another car full of guests, and departed in 15 minutes. Upon return to Martinsburg, a number of speeches were made and the train departed at 3:40pm to return some of the passengers to Altoona. The newspaper report provided the following route description, slightly edited to make things clearer.

> *The railroad from this place* (Hollidaysburg) *to Martinsburg is about fourteen miles long, and for picturesque and diversified scenery, will be considered unsurpassed by any of the same length owned by the Pennsylvania Railroad Company. The departure from this place into the Loop is pleasing and attractive, the crossing of the river to the mountain affords in an instant an entire change of scenery. The route along Short Mountain, with the reservoir stretching out like a beautiful lake on the right, fringed on the north side with the shadows of McCloskey's Ridge, is beautiful in the extreme. The road then enters the Gap between Dunning's and Short mountains. This is a very narrow defile, wide enough for the old pike, the Roaring Spring Run, the railroad, and Martha Furnace.*
>
> *The road takes the eastern side of the mountain and rapidly ascends until it reaches Upper Maria Forge* (a forge that operated 1828-1862 and located between McKee Gap and Roaring Spring). *As the slope is very declivitous* (having a somewhat steep downward slope), *great difficulty must have been experienced in getting a good bed. But there it is and solid as the eternal hill it skirts.*

The road then passes Lower Maria Forge (a forge that operated 1832-1876 and was located between McKee Gap and Roaring Spring) *owned by Essington Hammond, proprietor of Sarah Furnace and Franklin Forge. Then past Rodman Furnace* (two iron furnaces were built here in 1862 and 1872), *owned by the Duncan heirs but lately leased by Charles Knapp. At Upper Maria, the road by a bold span by a trestle bridge, forty seven feet high across the turnpike and the hollow, leaves the rocky ridge and takes the limestone bluff on the south side of the turnpike. This it pursues with still ascending grade till it reaches the paper mill, where leaving the Martinsburg turnpike and passing between the paper mill and the grist mill it meets the Woodbury turnpike, and leaving it to the west it makes up into that magnificent plateau of limestone land called Morrison's Cove.*

The grade from here to what is called the Summit on Erb's farm is very heavy, averaging eighty-five feet to the mile. Farm after farm of the richest soil is passed and away in the distant plain are seen the spires of Martinsburg, glistening in the morning sun. The summit is gained and then down by easy grade and Martinsburg, this loveliest village of the plain, is reached in a few minutes.

The line was initially very prosperous, and passenger service ran regularly. Much of the passenger service functioned as commuter service from Henrietta to Altoona – to Altoona early in the morning and back at night. A turntable and enginehouse were built at the end of the line to handle the service. The service remained strong until the Depression of the 1930s. For example, in December 1925, the PRR operated 4 roundtrip passenger trains a day from Henrietta to Altoona and back. Passenger service ended on August 25, 1934. Freight traffic after World War II also steadily declined and by the 1960s, trains ran on a very limited schedule.

By the late 1960s, the Pennsylvania Railroad merged with the New York Central, creating the Penn Central. This company soon failed and became part of Conrail in the 1970s. By the 1980s, Conrail was happy to sell off this line.

Note that every station and bridge location is identified by a milepost location, shown as a number in the left-hand column of the route guides. Railroads identify locations along their routes by mileposts, much like highways do. The mileposts date back from the construction of the railroad, and the distance is measured from various places on various lines. There are signs every mile along the railroad that identify this distance.

Everett #11 (2-6-0) at Rodman. Photo by Barton Jennings.

Morrison's Cove Branch
Duncansville Wye to Brookes Mills

6.2 DUNCANSVILLE WYE – The Everett Railroad has its office and shops on the south leg of the wye. There is barely room for the three house tracks, one of which serves the one-stall locomotive shop. The line to the west has been abandoned, leaving just a short stub towards Interstate 99, long enough to turn a locomotive and several cars. The Everett Railroad owns the south and west legs of the wye, while Norfolk Southern (NS) still controls the east leg.

Everett 1828 fills the mainline at Duncansville as it prepares to take a train to Martinsburg. Photo by Barton Jennings.

All of these tracks were once part of the Pennsylvania Railroad (PRR). This was the junction between the H&P Secondary Track to the east, the New Portage Secondary Track to the west, and the 6.2-mile-long H&P Branch north to Alto Tower at Altoona. This area is also known as New Portage Junction, located at Duncansville according to early PRR records.

Duncansville was created by Samuel Duncan and Jacob Walters. Actually, Samuel Duncan created Duncansville on the west side of Blair's Creek while Jacob Walters created

Walterstown on the east side of the creek. A community with two names caused confusion, and Duncan and Walters agreed to flip a coin to choose a single name. They met on the Blair's Creek bridge that connected the two communities to flip the coin. A large crowd observed the toss that led to the common name of Duncansville.

Duncansville was located on the Philadelphia-Pittsburgh turnpike and received the nickname "Irontown" due to the number of forges, iron mills and foundries located there. Other industries included woolen mills, wagon works, brick works, gristmills and lime production. The Borough of Duncansville was incorporated on March 4, 1891.

On November 6, 1916, an eastbound freight pulled by steamer #2736 was coming down the New Portage Branch from Gallitzin when the crew lost control. Reports indicate that it crashed into four steam locomotives here (#2477, #2759, #2665, and #971). The result was seven men killed, and 47 cars and five locomotives destroyed.

The milepost of the wye was once shown as 33.4. The new milepost is based upon the distance from Alto Tower. The grade crossing on the east leg of the wye – 3rd Avenue, also Highway US-22 – is milepost 6.15.

7.7 **HOLLIDAYSBURG** – The Hollidaysburg passenger station once stood to the north of the tracks on Broad Street, just west of the Newry grade crossing. Early photos show that it had a long, raised wooden passenger platform with a second floor in the center part of the station. Fire insurance maps show that this area was offices, with waiting rooms and ticket sales on the first floor. A separate baggage house stood just to the east. Several hotels, including the Hotel Antler, Kellerman Hotel, and Hotel Franklin, were across the street to the north. To the south, a spur track served the Hollidaysburg Roller Mills, and J.D. Law, a dealer in coal, hay, sewer pipe and cement.

Duncansville to Brookes Mills

Everett #11 (2-6-0), heads east through Hollidaysburg on a sunny November morning. Photo by Barton Jennings.

West of here and west of Lowe Street, was once the Thermic Coal & Coke facility, which also operated an ice plant. Today, the land is the Joe Kreatzman & Son scrap yard. Just west is the Poof-Slinky factory and warehouse. The company, formerly James Industries, has manufactured more than a quarter billion Slinkys, and still makes them in Hollidaysburg. During the early 1900s, this area was known as Gaysport.

Hollidaysburg was first laid out in 1796. It was named after the Irish immigrants who founded the community: Adam and William Holliday. The borough boomed when it became the main transfer point between the Pennsylvania Canal and the Portage Railroad in 1834. Its importance grew in 1846 when it became the county seat for the new Blair County. The closing of the canal transfer in the 1850s hurt the community and its population stayed around 2000 until the Pennsylvania Railroad constructed a large switching yard here in 1903. Later, the railroad built the Hollidaysburg Car shop to help ease the crowding at the nearby Altoona Shops. By World War II, the borough claimed to have a population of almost 6000.

Industries in the area included foundries and machine shops, a silk mill, car works, the railroad classification yards, and others to support the railroad. In the 1970s, Conrail built a car reclamation plant on the property, a facility that still operates to rebuild and scrap railcars. Today, Hollidaysburg's population is about 5800.

Much of downtown Hollidaysburg became the Hollidaysburg Historic District, listed on the National Register of Historic Places, in 1985. The layout of the streets and buildings has caused the area to take the name of "The Diamond," an area that today serves as a hub for various celebrations in Hollidaysburg.

7.8 **HOLLY** – Holly is the junction with the H&P, or Holliday Secondary. Many PRR timetables show this to be milepost 32.2. The junction is at the west end of the remains of the large PRR rail yard, on the west side of the bridge over the Beaverdam Branch of the Juniata River. The junction is a simple crossover between the two main tracks.

Just east of the bridge and to the south is the Canal Basin Park & Visitor Center. This area was once a busy port, as it was where the canal shipments were transferred from the canal alongside the Juniata River onto the Allegheny Portage Railroad to make the climb over the mountains to the west. In some cases, the canal boat along with its cargo was loaded onto the railroad. To handle the volume of freight, there were two large water basins located off of Bedford Street and Juniata Street in town. Connecting the two basins was once a canal lock, where boats proceeded into the upper basin along the Beaverdam Branch of the Juniata River. Wharves for local business also lined the waterway.

The Beaverdam Branch of the Juniata River forms near the Logan Valley Mall in the Altoona area by the merger of Mill Run, Burgoon Run and Sugar Run. It also collects the waters of Spencer Run and Blair Gap Run in its six-mile length. The Beaverdam Branch flows into the Frankstown Branch east of Hollidaysburg.

The Pennsylvania Railroad bought the Pennsylvania Canal and Portage Railroad in 1856 and built a new all-rail route. The canal stayed open for the next several decades, but was eventually closed as business dropped and flooding damaged parts of the system.

Alongside the park is the Hollidaysburg Team Track operated by the Everett Railroad. In this area was once the Hollidaysburg Iron & Nail Company. To the north of the tracks was the PRR Freight Station.

Everett 1828 builds its train at Hollidaysburg. Photo by Barton Jennings.

8.0 MORRISON'S COVE JUNCTION – Just east of the Juniata River bridge is the switch which takes the Everett Railroad around the south side of the once massive PRR yard complex. Located at PRR milepost 32.0, this is the junction between the Morrison's Cove Secondary Track (south to Morrison) and the east-west H&P Secondary Track. Look for the "End NS – Begin H&RS" sign.

According to the *Annual Report of the Secretary of Internal Affairs of the Commonwealth of Pennsylvania*, dated June 30, 1894, the PRR Morrison's Cove Branch operated 18.90 miles from Hollidaysburg to Henrietta. It also stated that the Morrison Branch from Morrison Junction was 0.70 miles long.

8.3 EXCURSION TRAIN STATION – Just east of Morrison's Cove Junction, the railroad passes under PA-36. On the west side of the overpass is the station building built to serve the passengers of the Everett Railroad's excursion trains. The station was built in 2015 to resemble a typical Pennsylvania Railroad depot of the area. The station features a ticket counter and gift shop, waiting room, and restroom facilities, and is located at 244 Loop Road in Hollidaysburg, Pennsylvania.

Hollidaysburg excursion train station. Photo by Sarah Jennings.

The five yard tracks to the north are owned by the Everett Railroad, bought 2009-2010 to serve as a yard facility. The railroad's Hollidaysburg bulk transload conveyor facility is located nearby. It can handle 120 tons per hour and is available at no extra charge for customer self-service.

Duncansville to Brookes Mills

Everett #11 pulls into the excurson train station with freight cars in the adjacent yard visible in the background. Photo by Barton Jennings.

8.7 **HOLLIDAYSBURG CAR SHOP** – Heading east from the train station, look for the sign into the DeGol facility. To the north are the last of the many railroad shops once located in Hollidaysburg, Pennsylvania. This complex includes the 1955 Samuel Rae Car Shops, renamed the Hollidaysburg Car Shop by Conrail. Tens of thousands of freight cars were built in Hollidaysburg over the years. Parts of the complex are still used for car repairs and scrapping.

Watco operates much of the yard and shop facilities as their GBW Railcar Services. In June 2014, the Greenbrier Companies and Watco Companies embarked on a 50/50 railcar repair joint venture called GBW Railcar Services, LLC.

8.9 **BEAVERDAM BRANCH JUNIATA RIVER BRIDGE** – After heading east through Hollidaysburg, the Everett Railroad curves across the Beaverdam Branch of the Juniata River to turn south towards Martinsburg and Claysburg. The Juniata River was an important area stream as it was the route of the Juniata Division Canal, part of the canal system of Pennsylvania. The river is approximately 100 miles long and this part starts not far west of here when a number of local streams flow together. It flows east into the Susquehanna River, and is its second largest tributary after the West Branch Susquehanna.

9.3 **LOOP** – The railroad crosses West Loop Road in this area as it makes a series of curves. The community of Loop is to the east, and the PRR once had a small station here.

10.1 **FRANKSTOWN BRANCH JUNIATA RIVER** – The Frankstown Branch of the Juniata River forms to the south at Claysburg where Beaverdam Creek and South Poplar Run join. The river flows generally north and east for more than 45 miles before merging with the Little Juniata River near Petersburg, Pennsylvania, to form the Juniata River. Claysburg is on the Bedford Secondary line of the Everett Railroad. A 1978 Conrail track chart simply labels the river a stream, and some topographic maps call it Halter Creek.

10.4 **RESERVOIR** – The PRR once had a small station here. The name Reservoir comes from the reservoir built in this area 1839-1843 by contractor Henry L. Patterson for the Juniata Division Canal. It was finally removed during the 1880s after the canal was closed, but some of the dam can still be seen to the west. During the lake's existence, there was a series of small resorts along its shore, including the Catfish House. When the lake was drained, the railroad leased the land to farmers.

12.2 **KLADDER** – Photos show that an ornate passenger shelter once stood here. Look for the grade crossing with Monastery Road. Just to the east is the Saint Bernardine Monastery, operated by the Franciscan Friars TOR (Third Order Regular). The history of the monastery states that the "Monastery building was erected and dedicated to St. Bernardine of Siena to honor .... it is said ... the patron saint of

Duncansville to Brookes Mills

the Minister General's delegate, Fr. Bernardine Russo who had proved a wise and friendly advisor to the friars. It was a proud occasion for the friars of the new Province when, in the summer of 1928, Bishop McCort, in the presence of a large crowd of clergy and laity, blessed and laid the cornerstone of the Monastery building. The first class of candidates was accepted on October 17, 1929." The history of the monastery mentions the railroad several times as a means of travel and a source for moving supplies and goods produced on their farm.

An excursion train pulled by #11 (2-6-0) passes the Kladder sign on November 19, 2016. Photo by Barton Jennings.

Little is known about the name, except that the family of Daniel Kladder once lived in this general area and that there is a Kladder Cemetery nearby. Somewhere in this area was reportedly a station named Stanfield, although it does not show on any consulted railroad materials.

14.1 BROOK – Historically known as Brooks Mill or Brookes Mills, this is the junction between the former Morrison's Cove Branch and the Bedford Branch.

Brookes Mills is located at 980 feet above sea level to the west of Short Mountain. The area was once known as Vicksburg, and several area churches still use that name. However, the Brookes Mills name came about due to the

Brooks Milling Company, which located here in the 1800s and manufactured winter wheat flour, corn meal, poultry and animal feed.

Brookes Mills is still a relatively small, rural community. However, Interstate 99 is just to the west with an intersection featuring a number of gas stations and a Walmart. Just south of the junction is the very large Walter's Auto-Wrecking yard, located between the two branches of the railroad.

Morrison's Cove Branch
Brookes Mills to Henrietta

14.1 **BROOK** – Turning to the southeast is the former Morrison's Cove Branch. Trains heading south now face grades as stiff as 1.64%.

15.0 **HALTER CREEK BRIDGE** – Over the years, paper mills along this stream polluted it beyond the limits of the local fish. However, recent efforts by Trout Unlimited have led to a cleaning of Halter Creek, and recently the sighting of brown trout in the stream.

Halter Creek forms on the east side of the Dunning Mountain, east of Claysburg. It flows north to Roaring Spring, through McKee Gap, and into the Frankstown Branch of the Juniata River just north of here. It was also known as Roaring Spring Run.

15.2 **McKEE** – To the west is Suburban Propane, a shipper on the railroad.

McKee, or McKee Gap, was named for the McKee family who lived in the area during the 1800s. A grist- and sawmill was built here in the 1790s by George Myers, who sold it to George McKee in 1810. While the town called itself McKee Gap, the railroad called it simply McKee, or McKee Station. A history of Blair County states that the station had an assigned telegraph operator and station agent.

Records also show that an iron mill once existed at McKee Gap. Named Martha, it was credited with producing 140 tons of iron a week during the 1880s, when the community's population peaked at about 1500. The original work on the forge took place in 1830 when Dr. Peter Shoenberger started construction. His son, Edwin, expanded the business by establishing the Martha furnace.

16.0 **RODMAN** – Rodman is located in McKee Gap and is named for the old Rodman Furnace that once stood nearby. The name Rodman originally came from Admiral Rodman of the U.S. Navy. During the summer of 1863, word was out that the Army of the Confederacy was heading north to destroy the iron furnaces in the area. With McKee Gap being an important route through the area, locals created an army to defend the gap. Colonel Jacob Higgins commanded the volunteers, and soon had a set of breastworks built across the gap. However, the "army" had no provisions and quickly began raiding area farms for food, earning them the nickname "The Chicken Raiders." Add a forest fire started from several cooking fires, and the total damage from the volunteers probably exceeded anything that would have happened had General Lee and his army headed here instead of Gettysburg.

This area is labeled as McKee Gap on topographical maps. They show the elevation to be about 1000 feet. To compass-north is Short Mountain, topping out at about 2075 feet. To compass-south is Dunning Mountain. Short Mountain and Dunning Mountain form a major north-south ridge with an elevation of more than 2000 feet. McKee Gap is the only major gap through the ridge in the area.

Everett #11 approaches the crest of the grade at Rodman. Photo by Barton Jennings.

Immediately to the south of KcKee Gap and to the east is the large PennStress manufacturing facility. PennStress acquired the former Newcrete division of New Enterprise Stone & Lime in December of 2014. Immediately to the south, the railroad has a siding to the east for loading ballast from the New Enterprise Stone & Lime works. A conveyor system brings the rock in from the quarry, often called the Roaring Spring Quarry. Reports are that the rock is seldom shipped off the railroad due to the many sources of rock in the area, but it makes great ballast for the railroad. The siding is often used to hold cars for the paper mill at Roaring Spring.

17.0 APPVION – To the west is the large Appvion paper mill, currently the largest customer of the Everett Railroad. The paper mill was originally built starting during the summer of 1865 by Daniel Mathias Bare, John Eby, and John Morrison. Operations started in 1866, but the mill soon burned from a boiler explosion. The mill was quickly rebuilt and paper production resumed in the spring of 1867.

In 1876, Jacob Cass bought one-third interest in the paper mill and the name changed to Morrison, Bare & Cass. In 1887, paper from the mill was being used in Bare's other paper venture, the Roaring Spring Blank Book Company. The October 1894 Sanborn-Perris Map Company map shows the paper mill to be the D. M. Bare and Company paper mill. To the east towards town was the Bare Milling Company, built in 1868 by Daniel Bare. By 1922, the paper mill was the D. M. Bare Paper Company. In 1946, the D. M. Bare Paper Company was purchased by Combined Locks Paper Company of Wisconsin. It became part of Appleton Papers through a merger in 1971, and then today's Appvion.

Appvion's website states, "We were founded in 1907 by Charles Boyd with nothing more than a boiler house and a small wooden building to our name. And we didn't even own the building. In the hundred years since, we've grown into a $700 million company with over 1,400 employees by embracing Boyd's vision to add value to paper by adding coatings to it." The railroad delivers chemicals and plastics to the mill, and ships out coated paper.

17.4 ROARING SPRING – Look for the former PRR station to the east. This is the south end of many excursion trains out of Hollidaysburg.

Roaring Spring station. Photo by Sarah Jennings.

Maps from 1894 show a station here, which by 1922 had become the freight house with a new passenger station (ca. 1905) just to the north. According to information in the Roaring Spring Historic District application, the "one-story brick building with hipped roof was built by the Pennsylvania Railroad for its Morrisons Cove Branch to serve the paper mill. Remarkably, it is the only historic passenger station surviving in Blair County." PRR caboose 477908 is displayed at the station.

PRR Caboose 477908 at Roaring Spring. Photo by Barton Jennings.

Roaring Spring was first settled during the 1760s when Jacob Neff built and operated a gristmill here. Edward Sanders moved here in the 1770s, buying the land around the spring about 1776 and slowly selling it off over the next several decades. By 1821, George Spang was operating a mill at what was called Spang's Mill. Daniel Bare and his son arrived here in 1864 and opened up a mill and mercantile business. He soon entered the paper industry. Plans were made to change the town's name to Baretown, but it became Roaring Spring in 1868 and was chartered as a borough on October 3, 1887. The name Roaring Spring came from the noise that the spring once made, but the sound decreased when construction to make the waters more useable took place.

For many years, Roaring Spring was very much a Daniel Bare community. Bare laid out Roaring Spring's first 50 building lots in 1865, providing a community for the workers in his paper mill. By 1886 the Blank Book Factory was built by Mr. Bare. After a fire, a new, two-story brick structure was opened in 1888. In 1900, a new three-story native limestone structure was built for the Roaring Spring Blank Book Company. The October 1894 Sanborn map showed that the Roaring Spring Planing Mill was just to the east of the station, with a coal shed served by the railroad. This mill was sold to D.M. Bare in 1897. Further to the east was and is the Roaring Spring Blank Book Company facility, now also the Roaring Spring Water bottling plant. D. M. Bare passed away in 1925, and was the subject of a huge obituary in the *Altoona Mirror* newspaper.

The Roaring Spring Blank Book Company received an additional 40,000 square feet of warehouse space in 1963. In 1977, the company expanded when it acquired a majority interest in Educational Aids, Inc. Today it still makes and sells products like coloring books, thesis and laboratory books, notebooks, and many other similar items. A unique product that the company makes is Roaring Spring Premium Spring Water, which it began to bottle in 1980. The company provides home and office delivered water and coffee.

Blank Book Co., Roaring Spring. Photo by Barton Jennings.

The train station and the area around it have seen a few changes over the past 30 years. In 1986, the Pennsylvania Department of Transportation removed the railroad trestle to the planing mill and rebuilt South Main Street to stay on the east side of the station and to eliminate a sharp curve. The station was acquired by the borough of Roaring Spring in 1988 from Conrail, and renovated with funding from a Keystone 93 Grant in 1995. The caboose was restored and displayed in 1992.

Roaring Spring Station. Photo by Barton Jennings.

The Roaring Spring Historic District was listed on the National Register of Historic Places in 1995. Much of the District centers on the pond created from Roaring Spring. Bare created the original park, and it has been expanded over the years. A stone arch was built in 1874 to channel the spring, and a breast dam was added in 1876 to impound the spring water into a pond. The dam was modernized in 1958. The population of Roaring Spring is about 2600.

Roaring Spring Pond. Photo by Barton Jennings.

17.9 BLOOMFIELD BRANCH – To the south is an abandoned railroad grade. According to the *Annual Report of the Secretary of Internal Affairs of the Commonwealth of Pennsylvania*, dated June 30, 1894, the PRR Bloomfield Branch once headed south from here 3.0 miles to Ore Hill. Ore Hill was the site of a large iron ore mine which supplied iron furnaces in Bloomfield, Martha, Rodman, and other communities. Ore Hill was named in 1845 after rich iron ore beds in the area.

The PRR built the line in 1873 to haul the iron ore, and a small station was built at Ore Hill. Peter Duncan gained control of the mine in 1903 and about ten carloads of ore were shipped out daily. However, the business didn't last and the railroad ticket office and agency were closed in 1907.

Business did pick back up on the branch for a few decades thanks to farming and logging. In 1922, a railroad siding and dock was built for a fruit shed to handle area apple production. At Ore Hill, the M. E. McNeal logging company had a 3-foot gauge railroad that worked the woods to the south. It used at least three Climax locomotives, including Climax serial number 1587, a B-30 class engine built in October 1920 for the logging company. A second Climax locomotive was reportedly built in 1911 to a gauge of 42 inches for the McNitt-Huyett Lumber Company, but it was regauged when sold to McNeal. The third locomotive was built in 1895 for the Ohiopyle Company and eventually became the property of McNeal. The lumber company later was based in Central City, Pennsylvania. In 1932, the train station was abandoned and sold for the lumber. (For those who have not heard of a Climax locomotive, it is a special type of geared steam locomotive designed to slowly pull trains over steep grades. They were manufactured in Corry, Pennsylvania, less than 200 miles away.)

Heading south from here on the Morrisons Cove line, trains are fighting a stiff grade of up to 1.60% for the next 1-1/2 miles. Somewhere in this area was once a station named Hoover.

18.9 **SMITH TRANSPORT** – Smith Transport provides various types of transportation services, as well as warehousing services. This is a recognized transload partner with the Everett Railroad, providing temperature-controlled storage, racked space, distribution services, 12 rail doors, and 50 truck doors.

On the south/east side of the Smith Transport complex is Edgemate. This company is a "manufacturer of quality veneer sheets and edgebanding products with an extensive inventory of Veneer species."

19.4 **ERB** – This area was once known as Summit and was located on Erb's Farm. For a number of years, the railroad knew this location as Erb. Heading to the southeast, the railroad makes a number of curves through a series of fields. Trains heading south suddenly have it easier as the grade starts downhill at an average of 0.5%.

20.1 **PECK** – Peck was the name of an important family in Duncansville, near Hollidaysburg. Today, it is the location of the Renaissance Nutrition feedmill. "Ren Nut" is the common name for the facility. The firm is a "full-service vitamin and mineral premix company," making customized feed primarily for the local dairy and livestock industry, but it also makes feed for swine, sheep, goat, equine and poultry markets. The railroad serves this mill on a regular basis, especially delivering citrus products to be mixed with the feeds.

Everett 1828 stops at Peck to deliver several carloads of citrus for the local feed mill. Photo by Barton Jennings.

21.1   CARGILL – Early on, the mill was known as Young's Feed Mill. Before 2013, this facility was owned by Pennfield Corporation. When the company went bankrupt, Cargill acquired the feed mill in January 2013. On August 30, 2013, Cargill sold the feed mill to Holtwood (PA) based Risser Grain, LLC. The sale agreement has Risser operating the grain elevator portion of the facility. Key State, based in New Enterprise, Pennsylvania, has been contracted to operate its retail agriculture business out of the facility and manufacture feed products for Cargill. Two spurs serve this plant, both switched from the railroad-north side of the mill. The elevation here is 1344 feet.

Just to the south of the Cargill mill is a large farm on the hillside to the southwest, full of tractors and other farming machinery. This farm is actually part of Cowan Equipment, a used farming equipment dealership that specializes in older and historic equipment.

21.5 **MARTINSBURG JUNCTION** – This is the north switch to the wye at the junction to Martinsburg. The Martinsburg Branch curves off to the east while the former mainline curves off to the south. **For details about the route into Martinsburg, see the Martinsburg Branch section on page 45.**

21.9 **HIGHWAY 2004** – The former mainline crosses this road, also known as Cross Cove Road, just south of Central High School. Freights often pull down to here to shove into Martinsburg for switching. The elevation is 1347 feet.

23.1 **BOSSLER** – About all that can be found about Bossler is that it was once a station on the PRR. The tracks are still in place south to Pennsylvania Highway 2006, and Bossler was somewhere in this area. On February 18, 1895, the Henrietta-bound train became snowbound near the Bossler station for almost three days.

   The railroad once went further, all the way through Curryville, Matthew's Summit, Page, and on to Henrietta. The grades on in to Curry ranged from 1.25% to as much as 2.00%.

24.0 **CURRY** – The railroad kept coming to Curryville – known by the railroad as Curry or Curry Station – to serve the Agway Fertilizer Blend Plant. Curryville has long been a center for dairy and feed products. Curryville first was recognized as a community when it was founded as a railway freight and passenger station in 1872. The name Curryville came from J. W. Curry, the first railroad ticket agent and station master. Curry apparently did a number of things, as a post office opened in the railway depot on February 7, 1877. In 1939, the post office moved into a nearby store, but moved back into the "new railway depot" on February 1, 1947.

The Curryville depot was apparently the center of the community. In the early 1900s, L. R. Over served as station master and the agent for the Adams Express Company. He also operated a general farm store, a warehouse, and enough other area businesses to be recognized as a "leading man in this section."

As stated, Curryville was very much based upon the local farm and dairy business. There have been feed mills here since the founding of Curryville, with the last being Agway. Others included Abbott's Dairy (opened 1917), Eastern States (1937), and Farm Bureau (1941).

The elevation of Curryville is 1427 feet.

24.8 **MATTHEWS SUMMIT** – There is little known about this station, but it was listed in the 1902 *Lippincott's Gazetter of the World* as being a station "on the Henrietta Branch of the Pennsylvania Railroad." It was still listed as a passenger train stop in 1925.

25.7 **PAGE** – There is little known about this station, but it was listed as a passenger train stop in 1925.

27.1 **HENRIETTA** – This was the end of the PRR Morrison's Cove Branch. The community of Leather Cracker was settled here and a school opened by 1795. Iron ore deposits in the area attracted miners, and soon a railroad. The community became Henrietta in 1870, named after Mrs. Henrietta McAllister, wife of Archibald McAllister. Archibald, representing Pennsylvania, was one of the few Democratic members of the U.S. House of Representatives during the Civil War.

The Morrisons Cove Branch of the PRR was extended to Henrietta on December 25, 1872. The railroad immediately opened a depot at Henrietta with a ticket agent, telegraph operator, and a track foreman. Daniel D. Morrell served as the first ticket agent. Daniel Morrell was important in the town as he also operated the local store, a shallow iron ore mine at Henrietta, and built a local dam as a water supply.

Being at the end of the line, the railroad had a turntable and engine house here. The turntable was enlarged in 1922 and the engine house burned in 1932. In April 1929, the regular passenger train was replaced with a gas electric car, but service ended on August 25, 1934. On February 27, 1941, the railroad received authorization to abandon the track between Curryville and Henrietta.

A post office opened here on April 4, 1872. Henrietta was incorporated in 1880 with a population of about 500. Railway mail service lasted from August 18, 1893, until September 16, 1917. The post office finally closed on January 15, 1935.

Government records show that there was an elevation benchmark on the Henrietta passenger station. Reports state that it was marked "Pennsylvania Railroad" and was located on a shelf in the rock of the foundation at the north end of the station. The elevation was listed as being 1394.54 feet, while Pennsylvania Railroad records show an elevation of 1394.37 feet.

Everett Railroad: History Through the Miles

Martinsburg Branch

The Martinsburg Branch is less than a mile long and was built to connect Martinsburg with the main line of the Morrison's Cove Branch. The Martinsburg Branch opened in 1872 as the line was being built east to Henrietta.

21.5   **MARTINSBURG JUNCTION** – This is the north switch to the wye at the junction to Martinsburg. The Martinsburg Branch curves off to the east. Many freight trains pull past the wye and back in to handle switching in Martinsburg, or to store cars on the line.

21.7   **ROARING SPRING PAPER PRODUCTS SPUR** – During the early 1990s, Roaring Springs Paper Products moved their school and office products operation to Martinsburg, taking over a former apple packing and canning plant, once used by Green Giant foods.

22.2   **MARTINSBURG** – A 1905 Sanborn map shows that the line into Martinsburg was double track and served several shippers. The Pennsylvania Railroad station was on the southeast side of the tracks, about 300 feet south of Allegheny Street. It was a rather simple wooden station with a covered freight dock on the south end. It continued in service as a freight depot after rail passenger service ended. The station was finally torn down in 1998. Just south of the depot and to the west of the tracks was a railroad water tower.

Across the tracks from the depot was the Johnstown Sanitary Dairy Company. It included a creamery and ice house. It did not have direct rail service, but used the dock at the station to ship out milk and cream. Just north of the dairy was the Klepser Brothers Flouring Mill, founded in 1898. Klepser Brothers also operated a flour and feed store in Altoona. In 1920, the Klepser Brothers filed with the Commonwealth of Pennsylvania for registration of their brands: Corn Chop, Cow Chop, and Horse Chop. Later records show that the brothers (David M. And Harry M.) were "proprietors of the White Lily Mills and manufacturers of Golden Dove flour and dealers in feed, grain, meal, hay and straw." Martinsburg Milling still operates in this area.

View of the mill in Martinsburg. Photo by Barton Jennings.

The first legal record related to Martinsburg dates from 1785 when John Brumbaugh had 1500 acres surveyed at what is today Martinsburg. On September 7, 1792, a warrant for the land was issued to Brumbaugh and signed by Richard and Thomas Penn. Located in the middle of Morrison Cove, Martinsburg became a "Post Town" in 1817. It was incorporated as a borough on April 2, 1832, and today remains the oldest continuously incorporated borough in Blair County. There is no clear explanation of the history of the name Martinsburg. Several historical markers at the edge of town state that it was named for Conrad Martin. The website of the Borough of Martinsburg states that it is "thought to be named for early cove pioneer John Martin."

The first train arrived at Martinsburg on May 6, 1872, greeted by a crowd from across Morrison Cove. A depot was soon built near what became Railroad Street. By the end of the year, the railroad had been extended on to Henrietta.

Everett 1828 works its train at Martinsville. Photo by Barton Jennings.

Everett #11 (2-6-0) at Martinsburg. Photo by Barton Jennings.

Bedford Secondary

The Bedford Secondary was a relatively late addition to the Pennsylvania Railroad (PRR) system. It was built to connect an isolated line to the main routes of the PRR. The first part of this line was built in 1871 as the Bedford & Bridgeport Railroad (B&B), 38.7 miles of track from Mount Dallas (PA) west and then south to the Maryland/Pennsylvania state line (milepost 76.7). There, the railroad connected to the Cumberland & Pennsylvania Railroad which reached Cumberland, Maryland. On the north end, the B&B connected with the Huntingdon & Broad Top Mountain Railroad and Coal Company which connected to the PRR mainline at Huntingdon (PA).

In 1873, the PRR opened their Dunnings Creek Branch from Dunnings Creek Junction (Milepost 45 near Bedford) northward to several ore mines at Holderbaum, Pennsylvania. An attempt was made in 1876 to build south into Cumberland by chartering the Pennsylvania Railroad of Maryland. However, the new company later became part of the Georges Creek & Cumberland Railroad, later the Western Maryland Railway.

The late 1870s saw several suggestions for the construction of a line northward to reach the Morrisons Cove line. In 1889, a Mr. Dudley and his son surveyed a route to fill in the gap, and soon issued bonds and began limited construction. At the same time, the PRR was working on plans for a similar project and extended its line from Cessna (Milepost 36, west of Holderbaum) northward to Imler (Milepost 27) in 1891.

By the end of 1891, the Dudley's funds ran out with much of the grading done. The company then failed and was passed into the hands of a receiver. Work began again and much of the rest of the grade was completed. After several legal issues, the Pennsylvania Railroad acquired the assets at a receiver's sale in September 1902. To complete the line, the Bedford & Hollidaysburg Railroad Company was created in March 1903.

Some track was extended from Brookes Mills to East Freedom, but little else was done until 1909. In that year, the Pennsylvania Railroad forwarded some money to the company to start construction, and crews started the work on August 9th. Construction on

Everett Railroad: History Through the Miles

the final dozen miles of the project included the grade over Queen, and the first train covered the line on April 17, 1910, hauling pay car #460 to pay the workers. On May 13th, an inspection trip operated over the line, hauling company officials, political officials, and several prominent local citizens. The line was formally opened on May 29, 1910. The line connected the Cumberland operations of the PRR with their mainline, ending much of the coal and freight moving over the Huntingdon & Broad Top Mountain Railroad and Coal Company. The Huntingdon & Broad Top Mountain Railroad declared bankruptcy on October 11, 1953, operated its last passenger train in November 1953, and ceased operations on March 31, 1954. The Everett Railroad began operations over four miles of track between Tatesville and Mount Dallas on April 1, 1954, providing local freight service to several shippers.

As the coal and iron ore mines closed, business on the PRR line also decreased significantly. A boom in refractory brick kept the north end of the line busy, but the PRR had little interest in diverting traffic to the railroads at Cumberland, Maryland. Until the early 1970s, the Pennsylvania Railroad operated tri-weekly freight service between Altoona and Cumberland.

In 1972, Hurricane Agnes tore out much of the track south of Bedford, and PRR freight service was cut back to Altoona – Bedford – Everett. The Penn Central changed little, and in 1982, Conrail abandoned the line south of Sproul, cutting off the Everett Railroad, and the tracks were finally removed in 1985. Today, the tracks north of Sproul are part of the modern Everett Railroad.

14.1 BROOK – Turning to the southwest is the former Bedford Secondary. A siding exists on the west side of this line just south of Brooks Boulevard, once known as Brookes Mills Road. The siding once extended almost all the way north to the Brook switch. The siding is often used to drop cars off when a train is working both lines. The main road entrance into Walter's Auto-Wrecking yard is to the east.

Just south of here at milepost 14.4, the railroad passes under Pennsylvania Highway 36. The railroad also crosses Cove Run using two bridges located just north of the highway. Cove Run flows to the north, entering the Frankstown Branch of the Juniata River north of Brookes Mills.

14.5   FRANKSTOWN BRANCH OF THE JUNIATA RIVER BRIDGE – This is reportedly the largest bridge built as part of the Bedford and Hollidaysburg branch of the Pennsylvania Railroad. Its construction specifications state that it is a concrete and steel structure having two spans of sixty feet each.

The Frankstown Branch of the Juniata River forms to the south at Claysburg where Beaverdam Creek and South Poplar Run join. It flows generally north and east for more than 45 miles before entering the Little Juniata River to form the main stem of the Juniata River.

Just south of the river bridge, the railroad also bridges over Everett Street using a through plate girder span.

15.2   EAST FREEDOM – Older PRR records show East Freedom to be at milepost 15.7. However, FRA records show that Freedom Street is at milepost 15.1, making a difference of about 0.5 miles in the mileposts.

Different sources claim two historic names for East Freedom. One historic volume states that, "East Freedom was first established as 'Three Forges' in Bedford County in February 1829." A second source states that East Freedom was known as "Johnstown and Bedford Crossroads." Both sources say that the community took the name East Freedom when Blair County was established.

Records show that Edward McGraw laid out a village plot here in 1839-1840 after a few buildings had already been built. A general store, saddle shop, shoemaker, inn and tavern, church, and a few other businesses were soon established on the west bank of the Frankstown Branch of the Juniata River. In 1840, a post office was established at East Freedom.

A simple wooden station once stood here, with a relatively long freight section and short trackside platform. In 1945, the station was shown on PRR records as a telephone office, but there were no station tracks or customers. The station stood until at least the 1970s.

Today, a short spur track is to the east of the mainline. On old Conrail track charts it is shown as the McClure Lumber track.

16.0   **INTERSTATE 99** – The railroad passes under the new Interstate 99, also known as the Bud Shuster Highway. I-99 consists of two small parts, one in central Pennsylvania and one in southern New York. This part started south of here at the Pennsylvania Turnpike (I-70/I-76) north of Bedford. It heads north to near State College, Pennsylvania.

The Interstate is called the Bud Shuster Highway for a good reason. It was the first Interstate to be numbered due to a federal law, this one Section 332 of the National Highway System Designation Act of 1995, written by Bud Shuster, then-chair of the U.S. House Committee on Transportation and Infrastructure. The numbering violates the Interstate numbering system maintained by the American Association of State Highway and Transportation Officials (AASHTO), as interstate highways are normally numbered south to north and west to east. In this case, I-99 lies east of I-79 but west of I-81.

18.8   **POLECAT HOLLOW ROAD** – This is the first public road crossing since East Freedom. Just south of here on the east is NPC, a large commercial printing operation. The firm started as a weekly newspaper and now is "one of the largest providers of print and information services to both the Federal government and commercial clients." The building has a rail spur to serve it.

19.6   **GENERAL REFRACTORIES COMPANY PLANT NO. 6** – In 1945, there was a large brickyard to the east. Brick manufacturing was a major industry in the Claysburg area. Several area mountains were covered with ganister rock, an almost pure silica stone. The refractory industry needed pure silica, and in 1883, Jesse Hartman began a silica quarry on nearby Sproul Mountain to supply his iron furnace. However, the real business of the quarry was the shipment of silica to various silica brick plants across the country. The silica brick was needed for the glass, coke, and iron/steel industries as silica brick could withstand temperatures up to 3150 degrees without melting or crumbling.

The first silica brick plant at Claysburg was built by Thomas N. Kurtz, with construction starting in 1913. The brick company, named Standard Refractories Company, produced customized bricks for the booming steel industry. Kurtz, who had experience working at other refractories, grew the plant to twenty kilns with a 140,000-brick capacity. In 1922, Kurtz sold his operation to General Refractories, which was already operating their plant at Sproul. With the sale, Thomas Kurtz used the money to gain control of U.S. Refractories in Mt. Union, Pennsylvania. He sold that plant to North American Refractories in 1930 and remained with that company as vice president until his death in 1938.

Plant No. 6 was a major shipper on the railroad. Brick often moved in large volumes for specific projects. Additionally, until 1951, the brick was heated with coal, creating inbound shipments for the railroad since it took 200 tons of coal to manually fire just one kiln. Beginning in 1952, the kilns were heated by natural gas. Employment at the brick plant took a large drop with the change to natural gas, but the plant continued to employ about 300 workers throughout the 1960s and 1970s. However, the recession of the late 1970s and early 1980s hurt the industries that General Refractories relied upon, and Plant No. 6 ceased manufacturing silica brick in 1984. The plant finally closed in June 1987 after attempts to make other related products. Today, General Refractories has only one plant making silica brick and it is located in Utah.

After the plant closed, a local trucking company leased the brickyard and established a warehousing operation in the company office building and storage sheds. The kilns, as well as the crushing and grinding building, were torn down. Today, the family-owned McCabe Group operates out of the site and specializes in warehousing, handling, and distribution of products. Their website states that they have "a capacity of 300,000 square feet of storage space, with 18 dock doors and 4 entrances for rail siding." The McCabe Group has partnered with the Everett Railroad to provide transload services for area shippers.

As the train passes the remains of the refractory – located to the east – the alley to the west alongside the tracks is Railroad Street.

20.3 CLAYSBURG – Early photos show two different depots at Claysburg. What was probably the first was a small wooden building, located on a spur to the east side of the mainline, built on stilts off the railroad's grade just south of the road bridge across Pipe Run. The station had a one-car freight dock and small bay window. A later photo shows a larger station, located on a wider fill. Several semaphores were located near the station, and across the tracks was a wooden water tower and water column. Today, this area is wooded, with a transload facility used by the McCabe Group to the west where the water tower once stood.

There are still short team tracks on both sides of the mainline. The one to the west was once the siding and the one to the east was the spur upon which the earlier stations were located. These tracks are the Claysburg Team Track, used for transloading "open or covered hoppers and tank cars of any size." The original Everett Railroad locomotive shops are to the west. A short siding is located to the west of the mainline, just a short distance south of Claysburg.

The history of the Claysburg area states that the first settlers were Valentine Lingenfelter and his two sons who settled here about 1770. The population grew after the Revolutionary War, and in 1804, John Ulrich Seth built a sawmill and gristmill. There was a movement of the community to the south in the 1830s when Dr. Peter Shoenberger opened the Sarah Furnace about a mile south of town. However, during the mid-nineteenth century, the

Sarah Furnace post office moved to Claysburg, which had become the housing community for the area. The completion of the railroad through Claysburg opened up the silica mines to the brick industry, and Claysburg and Sproul (Sarah Furnace) both soon attracted refractories. Between the two communities, almost twelve hundred men were needed to work the plants.

A shortage of labor caused the company to look elsewhere for help. By the late 1910s, African-Americans began to arrive looking for well-paying jobs. This led company managers to head south to recruit in the towns their employees hailed from. One recruiting trip was so successful that during World War I, the Department of the Interior reported that a trainload of African-American workers rode from Little Rock, Arkansas, to Claysburg. To house the workers, Standard Refractories Company, and later General Refractories, built and maintained company houses along Dunnings Highway and Bedford Street. The area, housing more than 150 African-American residents in the 1920s, became known as "Little Africa." Little remains of this area today as the houses and church were torn down as the plant closed. In the 2010 census, there were only seven African-American residents in a population of 1,625.

20.8 HOSS'S FRESH XPRESS SPUR – Just south of the grade crossing with Dunnings Highway is a spur track into the distribution center for HFX – Hoss's Fresh Xpress. The company is based here and was founded in 1988. Its local restaurant is Hoss's Family Steak & Seafood, and it also operates an outlet store.

Just to the south, the railroad has a grade crossing with Champion Drive, and then passes the Champion Homes facility where mobile homes were manufactured.

21.8 SPROUL – The Everett Railroad ends at Sheetz Way next to the large Sheetz Distribution Center. A short siding is to the west. To the east is a spur track, once the lead into General Refractories Company Plant No. 7.

Sproul began in 1832 when Dr. Peter Schoenberger built an iron furnace here. He named it Sarah Furnace after one of his daughters. The furnace operated here until 1882, attracting a post office. However, as the furnace went through a cycle of production and closure, the post office eventually moved to Claysburg.

With the opening of the railroad in 1910, Sarah Furnace again attracted industry. In 1910, the General Refractories Company built a silica brick plant here. The idea of the plant came from William A. Stanton, formerly employed by Harbison-Walker. Stanton persuaded seven other men to form a company to purchase the Sandy Ridge Fire Brick Company in Centre County, and to build a new silica brick plant at Sarah Furnace. Two more plants were bought over the next few years, all incorporated as part of the General Refractories Company.

One of the partners in the venture was Governor William C. Sproul, who served six terms as a Pennsylvania state senator and one term as governor (1919-23). He became president of the brick company, and soon Sarah Furnace was renamed Sproul. By 1917, the company operated 22 kilns at Sproul, and provided 68 company houses for its employees. The community's population was about 275 and there was once again a post office here, also named Sproul.

Plant No. 7 stopped manufacturing silica brick in 1960. It reopened in 1962, manufacturing specialty refractory products. This plant is now HarbisonWalker International. In 2015, the company changed its name. Formerly called ANH Refractories, which included A. P. Green Refractories Company, North American Refractories Company (NARCO), and Harbison-Walker Refractories Company, the company is now simply HarbisonWalker International.

Heading south from Claysburg to Sproul, the railroad has been climbing a grade ranging from 0.25% to 0.62%. The grade stiffened to 0.78% as it headed south from Sproul as it climbed to the top of the grade at Queen, just a mile to the south.

About the Author

For almost three decades, Barton Jennings has been organizing charter passenger trains and writing the route descriptions, both for planning purposes and for the enjoyment of the passengers. These trips have been from coast to coast, often covering operations that haven't seen a passenger train in decades. In addition, he has written a number of articles about various railroads for rail hobby magazines.

Bart has visited the Everett Railroad numerous times and has ridden the railroad from end to end, taking detailed notes about the operation and what can be seen from the train. He has been fortunate to get to know many of those who have known and researched the railroad. His basement has several rooms full of books, timetables and other documents about this and other railroads – important research items from a time long before today's internet. Today, Bart Jennings, after years working in the railroad industry, is a professor of supply chain management and teaches transportation operations. He also still teaches regulatory issues for the railroad industry, a way to stay in touch with the industry he loves.

This book is an outgrowth of all of these experiences and previous writings about the Everett Railroad. Much of the information comes from internal railroad records, government and public records, railroad workers, and conversations with old and new friends. It is hoped that you enjoy your adventure with the railroad and that this book is of assistance in some ways – *Everett Railroad: History Through the Miles.*

The author enjoying an excursion on the Everett Railroad. Photo by Sarah Jennings.

www.ingramcontent.com/pod-product-compliance
Lightning Source LLC
Chambersburg PA
CBHW050607300426
44112CB00013B/2112